Baby Farm Animals

Jane Katirgis

Bailey Books
an imprint of
Enslow Publishers, Inc.
40 Industrial Road
Box 398
Berkeley Heights, NJ 07922
USA
http://www.enslow.com

Bailey Books, an imprint of Enslow Publishers, Inc.

Copyright © 2011 by Enslow Publishers, Inc.

All rights reserved.

Library of Congress Cataloging-in-Publication Data

Katirgis, Jane.
  Baby farm animals / Jane Katirgis.
      p. cm. — (All about baby animals)
  Includes bibliographical references and index.
  Summary: "Introduces simple concepts about farm animals using short sentences and repetition of words"—Provided by publisher.
  ISBN 978-0-7660-3794-6
  1. Domestic animals—Infancy—Juvenile literature. I. Title.
  SF75.5.K38 2011
  636'.07—dc22
                              2010011895

Paperback ISBN: 978-1-59845-157-3

Printed in the United States of America

052010 Lake Book Manufacturing, Inc., Melrose Park, IL

10 9 8 7 6 5 4 3 2 1

To Our Readers: We have done our best to make sure all Internet Addresses in this book were active and appropriate when we went to press. However, the author and the publisher have no control over and assume no liability for the material available on those Internet sites or on other Web sites they may link to. Any comments or suggestions can be sent by e-mail to comments@enslow.com or to the address on the back cover.

✪ Enslow Publishers, Inc., is committed to printing our books on recycled paper. The paper in every book contains 10% to 30% post-consumer waste (PCW). The cover board on the outside of each book contains 100% PCW. Our goal is to do our part to help young people and the environment too!

Photo Credits: Shutterstock.com

Cover Photo: Shutterstock.com

Note to Parents and Teachers

Help pre-readers get a jumpstart on reading. These lively stories introduce simple concepts with repetition of words and short simple sentences. Photos and illustrations fill the pages with color and effectively enhance the text. Free Educator Guides are available for this series at www.enslow.com. Search for the *All About Baby Animals* series name.

Contents

Words to Know

donkey   **farm**   **horse**

Who grows up on the farm?

sheep

cow

horse

chicken

donkey

pig

ducks

goat

We grow up on the farm.

Read More

Elliot, David. *On the Farm*. Cambridge, Mass.: Candlewick Press, 2008.

Einhornew, Kama. *My First Book About Farms*. New York: Random House, 2006.

Web Sites

KidsFarm.
<http://www.kidsfarm.com>

National Geographic. Animals.
<http://animals.nationalgeographic.com>
Click on "Animal Photos.

Index

Guided Reading Level: **B**
Guided Reading Leveling System is based on the guidelines recommended by Fountas and Pinnell.

Word Count: 20